A Messy Mystery

Written by
Cath Jones

Illustrated by
Amy Jindra

Ransom

Sammy put her toy cars and her books away. Then she made her bed.

Now everything was in the right place. Her bedroom looked perfect!

"Gran, are you ready to go to school?" she yelled.

Gran jumped on her bike and Sammy jumped on her scooter. They raced off down the path.

"Have a lovely day," Gran said. "Work hard and learn lots."

Sammy had a fantastic day at school.

But when she got home, she had a big shock. Her bedroom was a mess! There were toy cars everywhere.

Somebody had been playing in her room and they'd been very naughty.

They hadn't put anything away!

The next day, after school, Sammy found the same thing. Once again, her bedroom was a mess. This time, there were books everywhere.

"I need to find out who is playing in my room," Sammy thought.

Sammy set a trap. She left a bucket of water in her bedroom.

The next time the naughty mess-maker came into her bedroom, water would pour all over them!

The next day, after school, Sammy found the same thing.

Her bedroom was a mess **again**!

There was water everywhere **and** her bed was unmade.

Her trap had not caught anybody!

Sammy told her friends, Silver and Flash, about the messy mystery.

"We have had the same problems in our bedrooms!" cried Silver and Flash. "**What** is going on?"

The mess was getting worse and worse. So Sammy, Silver and Flash made a plan.

On Saturday, Sammy said, loudly and clearly, "I'm going to play in the woods." Then she set off.

But Silver and Flash were in the woods, waiting for her. It was all a clever trick!

When Sammy joined Silver and Flash, the three little bear cubs crept back home.

CLUNK! BANG! CRASH!

"Listen! I heard something!" said Flash.

Had they caught somebody in Sammy's bedroom?

Sammy, Silver and Flash burst into Sammy's bedroom.

The room was **full** of granny bears!

"Gran!" Sammy cried in shock. "What are you doing?"

"You all have such splendid toys, books and beds," Gran said. "After we drop you off at school, we can't resist playing and reading and bouncing."

The three little bear cubs put everything away. Then they taught the granny bears how to be tidy.

"You can play with our things while we are at school," Sammy said. "But then you **must** put everything away! Agreed?"

"Agreed!" said all the granny bears. Then Gran did an extra bouncy jump onto the bed.